What Do Scientists Do All Day?

by Jane Wilsher

Illustrated by Maggie Li

WIDE EYED EDITIONS

Contents

Are you ready for an adventure?

Come with us and find out what scientists do...

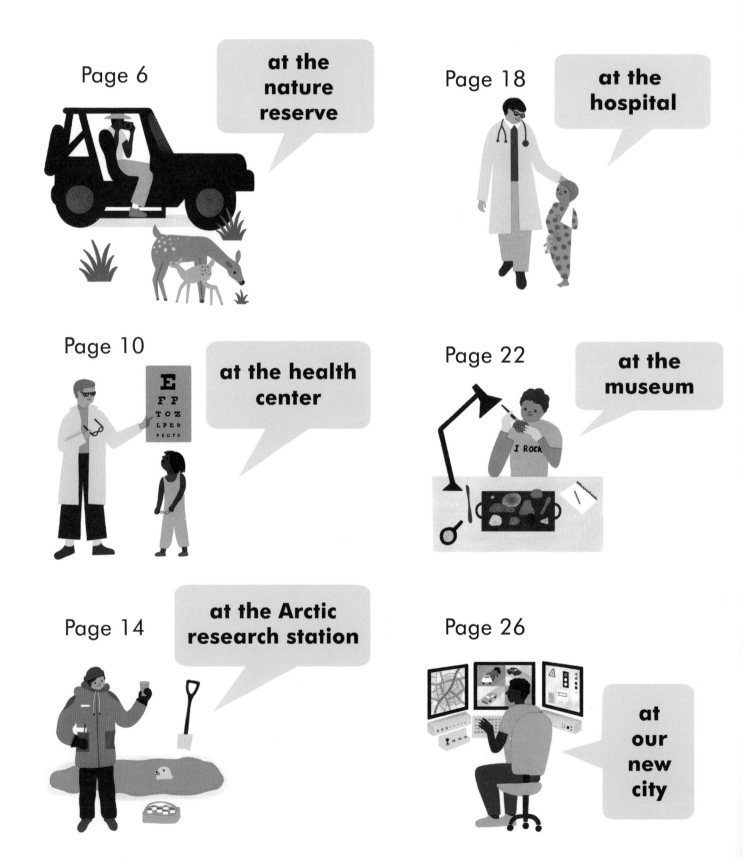

What do scientists do all day?

On this trip, we are going to tour 14 different places. After visiting each place, you can learn about eight special scientists who you will find there.

Then you can go back and try to spot each of the scientists in action. Can you spot them all?

What, why, and how? Scientists ask big, small, and tricky questions about our world. They test out their ideas with experiments, which often go wrong before they go right. Then they study the results to discover how things work.

But what do they do all day?

Scientists do all kinds of jobs. Doctors, dentists, and nurses help people, while vets look after animals. Archaeologists study ancient remains. Engineers help plan for the future. Meanwhile, inventors come up with brand-new ways of doing things. Whatever the job, scientists spend their days looking, thinking, and measuring, then planning what to do next.

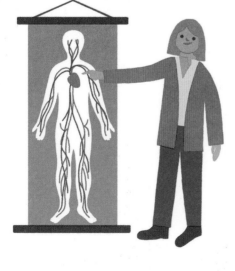

Welcome to the nature reserve

Take a walk among the birds and butterflies. Around every corner, there are plants and animals to spot. The team of scientists working here studies nature and cares for the wildlife.

What do scientists do at the nature reserve?

My job is to make sure that plants and animals can grow and live safely in the wild. I help to protect their homes.

Seeds are amazing! I study how they pop open and grow into plants. I watch plants change over the seasons.

Save our countryside! I show people how to enjoy nature and look after our beautiful world.

Water is everywhere, even in rivers under the ground. I test the water in all sorts of rivers to see if it's clean.

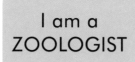

I study all kinds of wild animals. For my new project, I spend hours watching families of deer.

When the animals are sick, I feed them and treat them with medicine. I enjoy looking after the newborn animals.

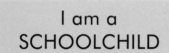

I love to watch butterflies. I take care not to frighten them. I'm making a chart of all the bugs and butterflies I see.

I'm a bird expert. I look at birds up close using binoculars. I wait quietly, out of view, in a hut called, a blind.

9

Welcome to the health center

Who's your appointment with? In each room, a different expert keeps you healthy, from head to toe, inside and out. Each person has a special job to do, from testing your eyes to polishing your teeth.

10

What do scientists do at the health center?

When you don't feel well, I find out what's wrong. Then I figure out how to make you better and decide if you need medicine.

I check and double-check. I prepare your prescription, which is the medicine your doctor tells you to take.

I'm called an audiologist. I check a patient's ears and hearing with machines. I fit hearing aids, too.

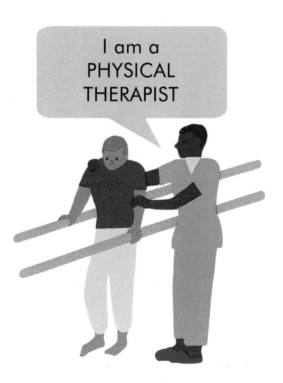

Let's move it! After patients have been sick or had operations, I help them to recover with movement exercises.

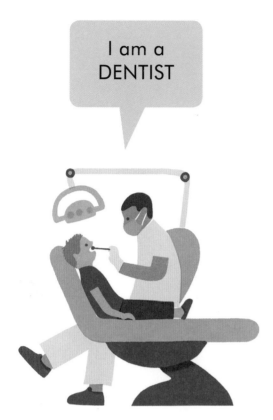

I am a
DENTIST

Well-brushed teeth make my day! I check my patient's teeth and gums to see if they are healthy. I treat tooth decay, too.

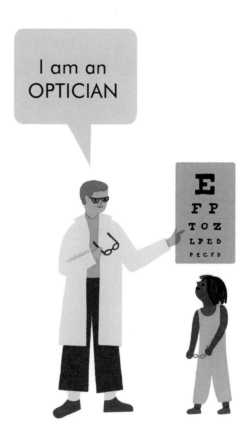

I am an
OPTICIAN

I test people's eyes. When someone needs to see more clearly, I find the best pair of glasses just for them.

I am an
IN-HOME NURSE

Often, I'm out and about visiting sick people in their homes. I check in on them and give them their medicines.

I am a
PSYCHOTHERAPIST

I listen and talk with people all day long. I help them to understand how they feel. We talk things through.

Welcome to the Arctic research station

Brrrrr! This is a freezing cold place at the top of the world. Scientists live and work here for months on end. They study Arctic plants, animals, and the thick, thick ice. The scientists work hard together to look after the Arctic.

What do scientists do at the Arctic research station?

I am a RESEARCH SCIENTIST

I study how plants and animals live together in the sea. I'm studying to become a marine biologist.

I am a MARINE BIOLOGIST

Sea plants and animals are my passion. I study them and check to see if their homes are being destroyed.

I am a RESEARCH DIVER

There's a world to explore under the ice. I look at how the animals live in cold water. I bring back water samples, too.

I am a TRANSPORTATION ENGINEER

It's freezing here! I make sure all kinds of machinery, including trucks and sleds, don't get frozen solid.

I study all kinds of animals, but polar bears are my speciality. I put tags on them to keep track of them in the wild.

I am a geologist. I take samples of snow, water, and frozen rock. I notice how things change over time.

We're alone at the top of the Earth. I keep us in touch with family, friends, and other scientists all over the world.

I love mountains and snow. I show the rest of the team how to work safely in this dangerous place.

Welcome to the hospital

You're in safe hands, here. Day and night, a busy team of doctors, nurses, and staff helps people to get better. Ambulances bring in emergencies. And babies are born here, too.

What do scientists do at the hospital?

I am a
NURSE

I give medicine to patients and change their bandages. I make sure they are comfy. We talk, too.

I am an
EMERGENCY
ROOM DOCTOR

Let's get you patched up! In an emergency, I'm the first doctor you see. I treat your injury or send you to a specialist doctor.

I am a
CHILDREN'S
DOCTOR

I help sick children get better. I work on a ward just for young people. Family and friends visit, too.

I am a
MIDWIFE

My job makes me happy. I help women give birth to babies. I try to make the moms and new babies feel cozy.

I perform operations. I look inside a patient's body. The best part is when the patient wakes up and feels better.

I work with the surgeon. I help the patient to fall fast asleep and not feel a thing while the surgeon performs the operation.

I'm a magician! I can see inside your body. I take special photos, called X-rays, which show if you've broken a bone.

I work in the laboratory. I test samples of blood under a microscope. The results help the doctor plan how to make you better.

Welcome to the museum

It's time to explore! There are fascinating objects, called exhibits, including dinosaur bones, a space rocket, and an ancient statue. Behind the scenes, scientists collect and study the exhibits.

What do scientists do at the museum?

I decide what we display in the museum. I help the museum team put on new exhibitions, or shows, for everyone to see.

I study dinosaurs and write about new discoveries. I also helped the team build our life-size T. rex model!

Bit by bit, I zoom in on tiny sections of an old painting. I repair the painting and try to keep it looking as good as it can.

I help to put on exhibitions about space. I make sure all the facts are correct. I give talks about space travel, too.

To find out how we lived in the past, I dig up, dust off, and study things left behind by our ancient ancestors.

I'm a time detective. I try to figure out the age of things. I test all kinds of materials in the laboratory.

I show children the really cool exhibits, plus the games and activities. I set the museum quizzes and search-and-find trails, too.

I'm on a school trip. I'm learning how to be a scientist by looking and recording information in my notebook. I want to be an astronaut.

Welcome to our new city

Let's build this city! There are jobs to do before the builders start. Each road, bridge, and building is designed to make sure it is safe and works properly. A busy city needs to run smoothly.

What do scientists do to make a new city?

I plan where new roads are built. I make sure the roads connect with railway stations and airports across the country.

I design new bridges and help repair old ones. The most important thing is to make sure each bridge is safe.

Under your feet, there's a hidden maze of pipes and tunnels. I build and repair pipes to carry all kinds of things underground.

"Safety first," I say. I make sure the places where we live, work, and go to school, as well as the machines we use, are safe.

Zip zap! I use an electronic tape measure. I make maps to show how the land is used and mark which plots belong to whom.

Drilling with a big machine is exciting. First, I test to see if it's safe to drill so I don't hit any underground pipes.

I hate traffic jams! I make sure the traffic flows smoothly. I use computers to set the traffic lights.

I plan the buildings everyone uses, such as airports and railway stations. I work with teams of designers and builders.

Welcome to mission control and the space station

This is an exciting place to work! On the ground, teams of scientists prepare, then 3, 2, 1! Liftoff! A rocket blasts deep into space. Astronauts dock at the International Space Station, which is a huge laboratory, where scientists study space.

What do scientists do at mission control and on the space station?

My job is out of this world! When a rocket is due to launch, I talk to teams on the ground and up in space to make sure everything is ready.

On the ground, everyone has a special job to do. We all help to make sure that the rocket takes off safely.

Each astronaut has a different job. I sit in the driving seat and fly the rocket into space. I keep in touch with mission control.

I'm an astronaut, and I look after the payload, or cargo. We're taking a machine called a satellite into space.

Come in! Can you read me? I'm in charge of the machines that keep everyone on the ground, and in space, in touch.

I map out the rocket's route and track it as it travels into space and back home to Earth.

I'm in charge of the International Space Station, where scientists from around the world work together on science projects.

I am an astronaut and a doctor. I'm on call if anyone is sick. I also carry out science experiments.

Welcome to the observatory

Look up at the stars! This is the best place to see the night sky. A powerful telescope helps scientists study the moon, stars, and planets to learn about our galaxy and beyond.

What do scientists do at the observatory?

I look after this huge telescope. It shows things far away and makes them look bigger. I check that all the parts work properly.

I'm fascinated by how the universe works. I use the telescope to study the planets, stars, and galaxies.

While pictures are beamed onto the domed ceiling, I tell the audience the story of what happens in the night sky.

I present TV shows about all kinds of science. I interview experts, too. I studied science at college.

I send and receive radio signals. I collect information to help make a picture of what's happening in space.

Space machines, called satellites, circle the Earth and send back messages. I figure out what the messages mean.

I'm writing a book about how to spot stars and planets in space. My book will be full of facts and new scientific discoveries.

In class, we do science experiments to find out how things work. We're here on a school trip to learn about space.

Welcome to the aerospace center

Keep an eye on the sky! Teams of scientists design, build, and test all kinds of aircraft. Then, thousands of miles above our heads, jumbo jets roar and helicopters whir. Prepare for takeoff!

What do scientists do at the aerospace center?

I am a
ROCKET
SCIENTIST

My job is cool. I design and test rockets! I make sure a new rocket can travel into space and land on Earth again.

I am an
AEROSPACE
ENGINEER

My job is all about aerodynamics, or how air moves over a flying shape. I design every part of an aircraft.

I am a
PILOT

I am a
COPILOT

I fly the plane. I work with the crew to take off from the runway. We cruise high in the sky, then I land the plane safely.

I help the pilot fly the plane. Before we take off, I check all the instruments. I keep in touch with the ground by radio.

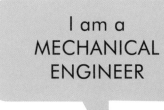

Whirr, whirr! I can tell from the sound of an engine if I need to fine-tune it. I design all kinds of aircraft parts.

Let's fix it. When a plane doesn't work, I find out what's wrong and repair it. I also service planes, by checking every part.

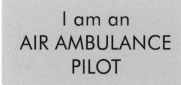

Emergency alert! I move quickly. I helicopter a doctor to a patient at the scene of an accident. Then I fly them to the hospital.

Cleared to land! I control the traffic up in the air. I keep planes a safe distance apart to avoid traffic jams in the sky.

Welcome to the botanical gardens

Season by season, the plants in the gardens change.
Walk through a forest, a vegetable patch, and
a hothouse full of exotic plants. The scientists
here study all kinds of plants and how they grow.

What do scientists do at the botanical gardens?

I am a
TREE EXPERT

I talk about how trees help to create clean air for us to breathe. I look after sick trees, too.

I am a
BOTANIST

When I'm not here studying plants, I'm on top of a mountain or in a swamp looking for rare, or special, kinds of plants in the wild.

I study CROPS

I am a
MEDICAL
RESEARCHER

I help farmers grow crops for us to eat. I test samples of soil and grow seeds that produce strong healthy plants.

In the lab, I study how some plants can be used to treat diseases. I test leaves, roots, and stems, then make them into medicines.

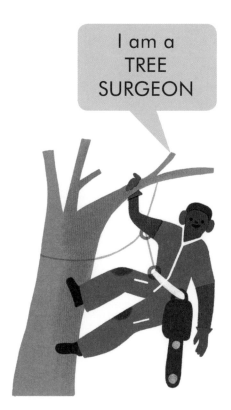

I like heights! I climb up a tree and dangle on a harness, then I cut away old damaged branches to keep the tree healthy.

Mushrooms are my thing! I travel the world looking for different types. Then I study them under a microscope.

I make PERFUME

Mmm, smell that rose! I mix different flower scents to make gorgeous potions. People call me "the nose."

I organize the library, which is full of books, magazines, and computer files about thousands of kinds of plants.

Welcome to the Earth Science center

Boom, crack, crash! The scientists here study
the wonders of our powerful Earth, from its
exploding mountains, called volcanoes,
to its crashing ocean waves and wild weather.

What do scientists do at the Earth Science center?

I am a
METEOROLOGIST

I watch the weather. I track clouds, rain, snow, and wind as they move around the globe.

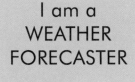

I am a
WEATHER
FORECASTER

Will it rain or shine? I use science to predict what the weather will do next. I show the weather as lines, called fronts.

I am a
GEOLOGIST

I study the Earth's rocky crust and how it formed. It is full of fossils, which are rocky imprints of ancient plants and animals.

I am an
OCEANOGRAPHER

I study oceans, from the frozen Arctic to warm tropical seas. I look at everything from waves to the shape of the seabed.

I look at patterns of weather, called climates. I study how life is changing as the world gets warmer.

I study volcanoes, which are mountains with hot liquid rock at their centers. "Sleeping" volcanoes might erupt!

I'm called a seismologist. The Earth's vibrations, or wobbles, cause earthquakes. I use a machine to measure the vibrations.

Water is vital. I test sea and river water to see if it is polluted. I study how water flows around the world, too.

Welcome to the energy plant

Flick a switch to power up! Machines need energy or fuel, such as electricity and gas. Scientists at the energy plant help electricity flow through wires and gas flow through pipes around the country and into your home.

What do scientists do at the energy plant?

I am the POWER PLANT DIRECTOR

I'm in charge. Every day, I read charts to see how much energy the plant makes. My team checks that the machines are safe.

I am an ELECTRICITY SYSTEMS ENGINEER

I oversee how electricity, which can be dangerous, is sent across the country. I make sure the network is safe.

I am a SOLAR POWER ENGINEER

I fit solar panels, which soak up energy from sunshine and turn it into electricity. I fix the panels to roofs to catch the sun.

I am a WIND TURBINE ENGINEER

I'm up here! I repair wind turbines, which spin in the wind and make energy that flows to the power plant.

I am a GAS SYSTEMS ENGINEER

In your home, I connect machines that use gas, such as a stove or a boiler, to gas pipes from the energy plant.

I am a RENEWABLES RESEARCHER

I'm studying how to use energy from nature, including the sun, wind, and waves. This natural energy is called renewable.

I am an ENERGY FUTUROLOGIST

I study new kinds of energy to make machines work. In the future, we need energy that won't harm our planet.

I am a NUCLEAR POWER ENGINEER

I make sure nuclear power is made safely. Atoms, the tiny building blocks of all stuff, are split. The energy they release is turned into electricity. The leftover waste is dangerous.

Welcome to the university

Studying science here is awesome! Teachers,
called professors, explain the wonders of science,
from how the body works to mind-boggling math.
Everyone shares their big ideas.

What do scientists do at the university?

I stand at the front of class and teach students how living things work, from top to toe, inside and out.

I'm training to be a doctor. At college, I study the science of the body. I also work at a hospital, where I help doctors.

Fizz, bang, pop! I study and teach how chemicals react with each other. I write up my projects in science magazines.

I ask big questions about how the world works, then I try to answer them by observing and thinking.

Numbers blow my mind! I use math to help solve problems. I work with scientists, engineers, and banks.

I study how we earn and spend money, including pocket money. I also look at how countries buy and sell things.

I'm fascinated by how people behave and live together. For my new project, I am asking lots of people "What's your favorite food?"

I study how the mind works, especially when people are unwell. I'm training to be a mental health nurse.

Welcome to the technology and computer lab

Techie magic happens here! Meet the brains behind the computers that keep us in touch. This is the place where robots are made and inventors come up with brand-new ideas.

What do scientists do at the technology and computer lab?

I am an INVENTOR

I'm full of big ideas. I come up with new ways of doing things. I invent machines and tools to make jobs quicker and easier.

I am a ROBOTICS ENGINEER

Robots rule! I design robots. I draw them in 3-D on a computer so I can see what the robot will look like from all sides.

I am a SOFTWARE DEVELOPER

I create new computer programs, from fun computer games to systems that help planes take off and land.

I am a COMPUTER CODER

I write code, or instructions, for the computer. My job helps you to see pictures and information on your screen.

My nickname is Mr. Connected. I help machines, such as a computer and a printer, "talk" to each other.

I'm a computer doctor. When a machine doesn't work, I repair it. I also stop it from catching viruses.

Around the world, all day long, people talk by phone and computer. I make sure all the communication systems work.

I make sure the sounds you hear in songs and movies are just right. I work at a sound desk and adjust the levels on dials.

Index of scientists

For Joe and Seth Wilsher with love —J.W.
For my team at OKIDO—M.L.

Brimming with creative inspiration, how-to projects, and useful information to enrich your everyday life, Quarto Knows is a favorite destination for those pursuing their interests and passions. Visit our site and dig deeper with our books into your area of interest: Quarto Creates, Quarto Cooks, Quarto Homes, Quarto Lives, Quarto Drives, Quarto Explores, Quarto Gifts, or Quarto Kids.

What Do Scientists Do All Day? © 2020 Quarto Publishing plc.
Text © 2020 Jane Wilsher
Illustrations © 2020 Maggie Li

First Published in 2020 by Wide Eyed Editions, an imprint of The Quarto Group.
100 Cummings Center, Suite 265D Beverly, MA 01915.
T +1 978-282-9590 **www.QuartoKnows.com**

A catalog record for this book is available from the British Library.

ISBN 978-0-7112-4978-3

The illustrations were created digitally
Set in Futura

Published by Georgia Amson-Bradshaw
Designed by Karissa Santos
Edited by Lucy Brownridge
Production by Dawn Cameron

Manufactured in Guangdong, China CC122019

9 8 7 6 5 4 3 2 1